TOGETHER AGAIN

Together Again

A Couple's Guide to Rekindling the Spark

B. VINCENT

QuantumQuill Press

Contents

Chapter 1

Chapter 1: Understanding the Spark

Characterizing the Flash: What precisely is the flash in a relationship?

In the complicated dance of adoration, the "flash" is frequently slippery yet irrefutably huge. Yet, what definitively is this immaterial power that lights enthusiasm and association between two individuals? In this part, we dig profoundly into the quintessence of the flash, investigating its multi-layered nature and revealing the unobtrusive subtleties that make it so dazzling. By acquiring an unmistakable comprehension of what comprises the flash, couples can all the more likely explore their excursion toward reigniting the blazes of energy and closeness. Go along with us as we set out on an excursion of disclosure, disentangling the secrets of the flash and revealing its groundbreaking power through connections.

Perceiving Indications of Reduced Flash: Normal markers that the flash might blur.

In the rhythmic movement of heartfelt connections, it's normal for the power of the flash to change. However, in the midst of life's intricacies, it's significant to remain receptive to the unpretentious signs that might flag a darkening of the fire. In this section, we enlighten the normal pointers that the flash might disappear, from diminishing actual fondness to a feeling of profound distance. By sharpening our familiarity with these advance notice signs, couples can proactively address hidden issues and set out on an excursion of renewal. Go along with us as we explore the fragile landscape of relationship elements, enabling couples to perceive and face the difficulties that undermine the liveliness of their association.

The Significance of the Flash: Investigating why reviving the flash is vital for relationship wellbeing.

In the embroidery of adoration, the flash fills in as a radiant string that winds around together, creating the texture of a flourishing relationship. However, past its surface appeal, the flash holds significant importance for the general wellbeing and imperativeness of the association. In this part, we dig into the ways in which reviving the flash is fundamental to sustaining a tough and satisfying relationship. From encouraging closeness and reinforcing profound bonds to reigniting enthusiasm and lighting a feeling of common perspective, the flash fills in as a reference point, directing couples toward more profound association and shared satisfaction. Go along with us as we enlighten the extraordinary force of the flash, rousing couples to focus on its safeguarding and development in their excursion toward enduring affection.

Factors Influencing the Flash: Outer and inner impacts that can affect the flash.

In the multifaceted dance of affection, the dynamic quality of the flash can be both supported and tested by a heap of outside and inward factors. From the tensions of day-to-day existence to individual weaknesses and unsettled clashes, these impacts can possibly either fuel the flares of enthusiasm or hose their sparkle. In this part, we investigate the unique exchange of these elements, revealing insight into how they shape the scene of heartfelt association. By acquiring knowledge of the powers at play, couples can proactively explore hindrances and develop a climate helpful for supporting the flash. Go along with us as we disentangle the intricacies of relationship elements, enabling couples to harness the force of mindfulness in shielding and reviving their association.

Setting Sensible Assumptions: Overseeing assumptions for reigniting the flash.

Chasing the flash, it's fundamental for couples to move toward this excursion with a feeling of authenticity and logic. While the craving to recover the wizardry of early sentiment is normal, it's essential to recognize that connections advance and change over the long run. In this section, we dig into the significance of setting sensible assumptions and treating optimistic dreams with a grounded comprehension of the intricacies intrinsic to long-haul organizations. By embracing the flaws and subtleties of their relationship, couples can encourage a feeling of acknowledgment and appreciation for the excursion they're setting out on together. Go along with us as we explore the sensitive harmony between desire and reality, enabling couples to leave on an excursion of rediscovery with clarity, empathy, and versatility.

Chapter 2

Chapter 2: Communication and Connection

Transparent Correspondence: Strategies for encouraging straightforward correspondence.

At the core of each and every flourishing relationship lies an establishment based on transparent correspondence. In this section, we set out on an excursion of investigation into the craft of cultivating straightforward discourse between accomplices. We reveal the fundamental methods and systems that prepare for certifiable articulation and weakness. From undivided attention to emphatic correspondence, we dive into the instruments that empower couples to explore troublesome discussions with effortlessness and compassion. By developing a culture of transparency and legitimacy, couples can manufacture further associations and lay the basis for a relationship based on trust and common comprehension. Go along with us as we disentangle the groundbreaking force of correspondence in cultivating closeness and reigniting the flares of enthusiasm.

Undivided attention is the specialty of genuinely hearing your accomplice and approving their sentiments.
In the racket of day-to-day existence, the straightforward demonstration of listening can frequently be ignored, yet it holds the ability to support significant association and grasping inside a relationship. In this section, we investigate the craft of undivided attention as the foundation of successful correspondence between accomplices. We dive into the subtleties of compassionate tuning in, focusing on the abilities and practices that empower people to hear and approve their accomplice's sentiments genuinely. From keeping in touch to offering intelligent reactions, we uncover the extraordinary effect of being completely present and participating in discussions with our friends and family. By developing a culture of mindful tuning in, couples can cultivate further sympathy, reinforce their profound bonds, and lay the basis for significant exchange. Go along with us as we leave on an excursion of revelation, investigating the significant capability of undivided attention to improve and breathe new life into close connections.

Remaking Trust: Techniques for Recovering Trust and Reinforcing the Bond.
Trust frames the bedrock of any getting-through relationship, yet it very well may be delicate and vulnerable to the strains and stresses of life. In this section, we dig into the many-sided course of remaking trust after it has been compromised. We investigate the diverse concept of trust, recognizing its significance in encouraging closeness and association. Through a progression of viable techniques and activities, we guide couples on an excursion of compromise

and recharging. From legitimate correspondence to reliable completion, we enlighten the pathways to reconstructing trust one step at a time, reestablishing the groundwork of the relationship to its previous strength. By embracing weakness and responsibility, couples can rise above past treacheries and become more grounded, fashioning a bond grounded in validity and common regard. Go along with us as we explore the fragile landscape of trust, enabling couples to develop strength and mettle notwithstanding misfortune.

Quality Time Together: Focusing on significant minutes to extend association.

In the hurrying around of present-day life, it's easy for couples to become cleared up in the hurricane of obligations, practically ruling out significant associations. Nonetheless, in the midst of the disarray, cutting out quality time together is central to sustaining the connection between accomplices. In this part, we investigate the significance of focusing on significant snapshots of harmony. From cozy meals to unconstrained undertakings, we dig into inventive ways for couples to develop shared encounters that extend their association and reignite the flash. By saving devoted time for one another, couples can encourage closeness, reinforce their profound security, and make valued memories that support them through life's difficulties. Go along with us as we leave on an excursion of disclosure, uncovering the groundbreaking force of time in cultivating perseverance through affection and association.

Closeness Past Physical: Investigating profound closeness and its job in reigniting the flash.

While actual closeness is often celebrated as the foundation of heartfelt association, profound closeness really supports and develops the connection between accomplices. In this part, we set out on an excursion of investigation into the rich embroidery of close-to-home closeness, revealing its significant importance in reigniting the flash in a relationship. We dive into the complexities of weakness, compassion, and legitimate association, enlightening the pathways to developing profound closeness. From sharing expectations and fears to offering backing and approval, we investigate the heap manners by which couples can support closeness beyond the actual domain. By cultivating a profound sense of close-to-home association, couples can reignite the blazes of energy, invigorate their security, and create a relationship that blossoms with shared understanding and significant association. Go along with us as we disentangle the extraordinary force of close-to-home closeness, enabling couples to develop an adoration that rises above the physical and perseveres through the preliminaries of time.

Chapter 3

Chapter 3: Rediscovering Romance

Reproducing Date Evenings: Creative thoughts for paramount date evenings to reignite sentiment.

In the midst of the requests of day-to-day existence, cutting out time for sentiment can frequently feel like an overwhelming errand. However, in the midst of the turmoil, the custom of date evenings fills in as an encouraging sign, offering couples a consecrated space to reconnect and rediscover the sorcery of adoration. In this part, we leave on an excursion of investigation into the craft of reproducing date evenings. From cozy meals under the stars to bold outings to new districts, we uncover imaginative plans to implant sentiment back into the relationship. Whether it's a comfortable night at home or an adrenaline-energized caper, we offer motivation and reasonable ways to make important encounters that reignite energy and extend association. Go along with us as we explore the landscape of sentiment, engaging couples to make loved moments that support them through life's highs and lows.

Shock Motions and Gifts: Little thoughtful gestures to show love and appreciation.
In the embroidered artwork of adoration, it's generally expected that the little, unforeseen signals that weave the most get through the strings of association. In this section, we investigate the groundbreaking force of shock signals and gifts in reigniting sentiment in a relationship. From written by hand love notes to surprising spots to smart badges of appreciation, we dig into the heap of manners by which little thoughtful gestures can say a lot of adoration. Through a progression of functional ideas and genuine tales, we encourage couples to mix their relationship with immediacy and mindfulness. By embracing the delight of giving and getting shocks, couples can develop a feeling of expectation and enjoyment, cultivating a more profound bond and reigniting the fire of sentiment. Go along with us as we set out on an excursion of disclosure, uncovering the sorcery of shock signals in keeping love alive and flourishing.

Main avenues for affection include seeing each other's ways to express affection and communicating love.
In the complicated dance of adoration, correspondence takes on many structures, each pervaded with its own one-of-a kind language of articulation. In this section, we dig into the extraordinary idea of main avenues for affection, spearheaded by relationship master Gary Chapman. By getting it and communicating in our accomplice's way to express affection, we open the way to more profound association and closeness. Through a progression of pragmatic

activities and wise stories, we guide couples on an excursion of self-revelation, assisting them with distinguishing their essential main avenues for affection and those of their accomplice. Furnished with this information, couples can tailor their demeanors of adoration and warmth in manners that reverberate profoundly with their accomplice's heart. Whether it's through demonstrations of administration, uplifting statements, quality time, actual touch, or getting gifts, we investigate how couples can really impart love in manners that feed and support their relationship. Go along with us as we disentangle the secrets of ways to express affection, enabling couples to communicate in the language of adoration easily and legitimately.

Suddenness and Experience: Embracing immediacy to infuse energy into the relationship.

In the cadence of regular daily existence, routine can frequently turn into the adversary of sentiment, smothering the feeling of suddenness and experience that powers energy and fervor. In this part, we leave on an excursion of investigation into the extraordinary force of immediacy in reigniting the flash in a relationship. We dive into the specialty of embracing the unforeseen, quickly taking advantage of opportunities to inject fervor and oddity into the association. From unconstrained travels to extemporaneous picnics in the recreation area, we offer motivation and viable ways to infuse a feeling of experience into our day-to-day existence. By venturing beyond their usual ranges of familiarity and embracing the obscure, couples can rediscover the adventure of revelation and make loved recollections that tight spot them together. Go along with us as we explore the thrilling landscape of immediacy, enabling couples to break free from the shackles of routine and embrace the delight of suddenness in their excursion toward enduring affection.

Developing Shared Interests: Tracking down new leisure activities or returning to old ones together.
In the rich embroidery of affection, shared interests act as the strings that tighten couples together, cultivating a feeling of kinship and association. In this section, we investigate the groundbreaking capability of developing shared leisure activities and interests for the purpose of extending closeness and reigniting the flash in a relationship. From investigating new interests together to returning to old side interests from the beginning of romance, we dive into the ways in which shared exercises can enhance the connection between accomplices. Whether it's cooking together, leaving on open-air undertakings, or seeking after imaginative undertakings, we propose down-to-earth thoughts and ardent accounts to move couples to investigate new roads of shared pleasure. By cultivating a sense of joint effort and common investigation, couples can create a sense of mutual perspective and experience that empowers their relationship and fortifies their association. Go along with us as we set out on an excursion of revelation, revealing the delight and satisfaction that anticipate couples who try to investigate the world together inseparably.

Chapter 4: Nurturing Emotional Connection

Weakness and Realness: Building a place of refuge for weakness and credible articulation.

In the safe-haven of a caring relationship, weakness is definitely not an indication of shortcoming but rather a demonstration of the strength of the connection between accomplices. In this part, we leave on a significant investigation of weakness and realness as the foundations of close-to-home association. We dive into the extraordinary force of opening up and sharing our most profound considerations, fears, and wants with our accomplice, making a consecrated space where trustworthiness and credibility flourish. Through functional activities and sincere stories, we guide couples on an excursion of self-disclosure, enabling them to embrace weakness as a pathway to more profound closeness and association. By developing a culture of transparency and acknowledgment, couples can lay the groundwork for a relationship grounded in trust, common comprehension, and unqualified love. Go along with us as we disentangle the secrets of weakness, welcoming couples to gallantly step into the profundities of their souls and fashion a security that rises above the common.

Basic encouragement: being there for one another during testing times.

In the mind-boggling dance of affection, everyday encouragement fills in as a life saver, offering comfort and strength during life's unavoidable hardships. In this section, we dive into the significant significance of being there for one another during moments of misfortune. We investigate the craft of undivided attention, offering an empathetic ear and a shoulder to rest on when our accomplice is out of luck. Through viable direction and genuine tales, we enable couples to develop a culture of compassion and backing inside their relationship. By encouraging a climate where weakness is met with understanding and sympathy, couples can endure the hardships of coexistence, arising more grounded and more joined than at any time in recent memory. Go along with us as we set out on an excursion of profound association, commending the extraordinary force of unqualified help in sustaining perseverance through affection and versatility.

Pardoning and Giving Up: Delivering Past Complaints to Push Forward in the Relationship.

In the embroidery of affection, pardoning is a string that ties couples together, winding around a way toward mending and compromise. In this section, we investigate the significant meaning of pardoning and giving up in sustaining profound associations within a relationship. We dive into the intricacies of clutching past complaints, recognizing the weight it puts on the connection between accomplices. Through sincere tales and down-to-earth systems, we guide couples on an excursion of pardoning, offering instruments to deliver disdain and develop a feeling of empathy and understanding. By embracing pardoning as an extraordinary demonstration of adoration and self-safeguarding, couples can break free from the chains of hatred and leave on an excursion of reestablishment and compromise. Go along with us as we explore the landscape of pardoning, enabling couples to relinquish the past and embrace a future loaded with adoration, sympathy, and trust.

Appreciation and Appreciation: Recognizing the positive parts of your accomplice and relationship.
In the buzzing about of our day-to-day existence, it's not difficult to underestimate the favors of our relationship, ignoring the little signals and characteristics that make our accomplice really unique. In this section, we leave on an excursion of appreciation, investigating the groundbreaking force of recognizing the positive parts of our accomplice and relationship. We dive into the act of developing a feeling of appreciation, commending the extraordinary character-istics and commitments that our accomplice brings to our lives. Through pragmatic activities and sincere reflections, we guide couples on an excursion of revelation, empower-ing them to communicate appreciation for one another's assets, kindnesses, and endeavors. By cultivating a culture of appreciation inside their relationship, couples can sup-port a profound feeling of association and satisfaction, en-couraging a bond that develops further as time passes. Go

along with us as we embrace the force of appreciation, enabling couples to develop a relationship loaded with affection, bliss, and appreciation.

Developing Sympathy: Understanding and sympathizing with one another's viewpoints.

In the mind-boggling embroidery of adoration, compassion fills in as the brilliant string that winds around the hearts of accomplices, encouraging a profound feeling of understanding and association. In this section, we dive into the groundbreaking force of compassion in supporting close-to-home associations within a relationship. We investigate the specialty of venturing into our accomplice's perspective, trying to grasp their contemplations, sentiments, and encounters with sympathy and compassion. Through pragmatic activities and sincere tales, we guide couples on an excursion of compassion, offering devices to overcome any barrier between contrasting points of view and develop a more profound sense of closeness. By embracing sympathy as the foundation of their relationship, couples can rise above errors and clashes, producing a bond grounded in shared understanding and acknowledgment. Go along with us as we set out on an excursion of close-to-home association, praising the extraordinary force of compassion in sustaining perseverance through affection and association.

Chapter 5: Overcoming Challenges Together

Compromise: solid ways of tending to clashes and conflicts.

In the complex dance of affection, clashes and conflicts are unavoidable, yet how couples explore these difficulties can significantly impact the wellbeing and life span of their relationship. In this section, we leave on an excursion of investigation into the craft of compromise, enlightening the pathways to helpful discourse and common comprehension. We dig into the significance of undivided attention, sympathy, and powerful correspondence in raising struggles and figuring out something worth agreeing on. Through useful procedures and genuine stories, we enable couples to move toward conflict as an open door for development and more profound association. By encouraging a culture of regard and splitting the difference, couples can change struggle into a chance for reinforcing their bond and sustaining a relationship based on trust and shared regard. Go along with us as we explore the landscape of compromise, enabling couples to explore the unavoidable difficulties of adoration with beauty, strength, and empathy.

Overseeing Pressure: Methods for dealing with especially difficult times for exploring unpleasant circumstances collectively.

Life's process is frequently laden with difficulties and stressors that can overburden even the most grounded of connections. In this part, we investigate the significance of overseeing pressure as a team, offering functional methodologies for exploring tough spots with versatility and effortlessness. We dig into the craft of encouraging a strong climate where accomplices can rest on one another for strength and comfort during seasons of difficulty. From rehearsing care and taking care of oneself to participating in open correspondence and critical thinking, we give couples the devices they need to face life's hardships together. By embracing pressure as a chance for development and association, couples can rise out of testing circumstances with a more profound bond and a recharged sense of direction. Go along with us as we set out on an excursion of flexibility, engaging couples to confront life's difficulties with boldness, solidarity, and faithful help for one another.

Adjusting Singularity and Fellowship: Keeping up with Freedom While Encouraging Areas of Strength for.

In the mind-boggling dance of adoration, finding the sensitive harmony among uniqueness and fellowship is fundamental for the wellbeing and imperativeness of a relationship. In this section, we dig into the specialty of keeping up with freedom while supporting areas of strength for a firm organization. We investigate the significance of respecting each other's exceptional characters, interests, and desires while likewise developing a profound sense of association and solidarity as a team. Through common-sense direction and ardent accounts, we enable couples to explore the intricacies of offsetting individual indepen-dence with shared objectives and values. By cultivating a culture of common regard, understanding, and backing, couples can create a relationship dynamic where the two accomplices feel esteemed, insisted on, and allowed to seek after their singular ways while likewise improving their co-existence. Go along with us as we set out on an excursion of congruity and solidarity, commending the magnificence of uniqueness inside the system of a cherishing and steady organization.

Looking for Proficient Assistance: When and How to Think About Couples Treatment or Guidance.

In the excursion of affection, there might come times when couples experience difficulties that seem impossible all alone. In this section, we investigate the priceless asset of couples treatment or direction by exploring complex issues and reinforcing the underpinnings of the relationship. We dive into the signs that might demonstrate the requirement for proficient mediation, like repeating clashes, correspon-dence breakdowns, or unsettled close-to-home injuries. Through pragmatic direction and empathetic knowledge, we engage couples to conquer any disgrace or delay encom-passing treatment, remembering it as a proactive move to-ward mending and development. By embracing the help and direction of a prepared professional, couples can acquire new points of view, foster powerful relational abilities, and manufacture further associations with one another. Go along with us as we set out on an excursion of self-revelation and mending, commending the extraordinary force of treatment in encouraging getting through affection and strength.

Building up Responsibility: Restoring promises and re-affirming commitment to one another.

In the embroidered artwork of affection, responsibility is the durable string that ties couples together through the preliminaries and wins of life. In this section, we investigate the meaning of reaffirming and reinforcing responsibility for the purpose of strengthening the connection between accomplices. We dive into the force of recharging functions, where couples can meet up to consider their excursion, offer thanks for one another's presence in their lives, and commit once again to the commitments they made to each other. Through genuine customs and representative motions, couples can reignite the fire of energy and re-affirm their commitment to one another's satisfaction and prosperity. By embracing the sacrosanct commitments of adoration and loyalty, couples can develop a relationship grounded in trust, common regard, and immovable dedication. Go along with us as we commend the magnificence of responsibility, engaging couples to sustain an affection that endures over the extreme long haul and twists as time passes.

Chapter 6: Sustaining the Spark

Nonstop Development and Picking Up: Embracing individual and social development for long-haul imperativeness. In the consistently developing excursion of adoration, stagnation is the foe of essentialness. In this section, we dive into the groundbreaking force of nonstop development and advancement as fundamental elements for supporting the flash in a relationship. We investigate the significance of embracing self-awareness and social development for the purpose of extending closeness and association. Through a promise to self-revelation, couples can uncover new features of themselves and their organization, cultivating a feeling of interest and fervor that keeps the fire of enthusiasm alive. By sustaining a development mentality and a readiness to advance together, couples can explore the rhythmic movements of existence with strength and effortlessness, arising more grounded and more associated than any time in recent memory. Go along with us as we set out on an excursion of investigation and development, praising the magnificence of development in affection and connections.

Customary Relationship Registrations: Making space to evaluate and support the relationship.

In the hurrying around of day-to-day existence, it's easy for couples to fail to focus on the advancing elements inside their relationship. In this part, we investigate the significance of ordinary relationship registrations as an imperative practice for supporting the flash and cultivating social wellbeing. We dig into the specialty of cutting out purposeful chances to evaluate the condition of the relationship, permitting couples to transparently convey their requirements, wants, and worries in a protected and steady climate. Through directed conversations and intelligent activities, couples can acquire knowledge about the qualities and regions for development inside their association, laying the foundation for significant exchange and association. By focusing on these customary registrations, couples can proactively address any difficulties that emerge, support a more profound comprehension of one another, and reaffirm their obligation to the relationship. Go along with us as we set out on an excursion of self-revelation and common investigation, engaging couples to develop a relationship that flourishes with open correspondence, trust, and weakness.

Adaptability and Flexibility: Acclimating to life changes and difficulties together.

Life is an excursion loaded up with exciting bends in the road, giving couples a horde of difficulties and opening doors for development. In this part, we dive into the craft of adaptability and versatility as fundamental abilities for exploring the steadily changing scene of life collectively. We investigate the significance of embracing change with an open heart and a feeling of versatility, perceiving that the capacity to adjust is vital to supporting the flash in a relationship. Through commonsense direction and ardent tales, we engage couples to move toward life's vulnerabilities as any open doors for shared development and investigation. By developing a mentality of adaptability and versatility, couples can face any hardship with effortlessness and solidarity, arising more grounded and more associated on the opposite side. Go along with us as we leave on an excursion of change, commending the magnificence of flexibility and versatility in affection and connections.

Observing Achievements: Recognizing accomplishments and achievements as a team.

In the embroidery of affection, it's fundamental to stop and commend the achievements that mark the excursion of a relationship. In this section, we investigate the extraordinary force of recognizing and regarding accomplishments, both of all shapes and sizes, as a team. We dig into the significance of making customs to honor extraordinary minutes, from commemorations and advancements to individual triumphs and shared achievements. Through purposeful demonstrations of festivity and reflection, couples can extend their bond and make enduring recollections that support them through the highs and lows of life. By getting some margin to respect each other's accomplishments and achievements, couples can develop a feeling of appreciation and shared help that reinforces their association and recharges their obligation to one another. Go along with us as we leave on an excursion of festivity, praising the excellence of adoration and organization in the entirety of its structures.

Appreciation Work on: developing a mentality of appreciation for one another and the relationship.

In the midst of the tumult of daily existence, it is not entirely obvious what gifts encompass us, including the affection and backing of our accomplice. In this part, we investigate the extraordinary force of appreciation as training for supporting the flash in a relationship. We dive into the specialty of developing a mentality of appreciation and gratitude for one another and the relationship in general. Through straightforward yet significant everyday practices like keeping an appreciation diary, communicating verbal appreciation, or performing thoughtful gestures, couples can cultivate a more profound feeling of association and happiness. By zeroing in on the positive parts of their organization and offering thanks for one another's presence in their lives, couples can gradually expand the influence of adoration and energy that improves each part of their relationship. Go along with us as we set out on an excursion of appreciation, praising the magnificence of affection and organization in the entirety of its structures.